Lord Deliver Me

Lord Deliver Me

Carlos Turner

J. Kenkade
PUBLISHING®
LITTLE ROCK, ARKANSAS

J. Kenkade Publishing
6104 Forbing Rd
Little Rock, AR 72209
www.jkenkadepublishing.com
Facebook.com/jkenkadepublishing

J. Kenkade Publishing is a registered trademark.

Printed in the United States of America
ISBN 978-1-944486-91-4

Table of Contents

INTRODUCTION

One day, I was watching a video of a deer stuck in a fence. In the video, he is trying his very best to get untangled. There's no telling how long he's been in that position, but he never stops kicking and trying to get out because he knows his life depends on it. Besides that, he just wants to get on with his life. Then, suddenly, a man jumps out of his truck and grabs the deer to calm him down. The deer is kicking like somebody is attacking him. Finally, the deer calms down, and the man begins to untangle the deer from the wires of the fence.

After about twenty minutes of tussling, bam! There goes the deer, free and delivered from what kept him stuck, bound, hindered, and so forth. It reminded me of how many people are stuck, bound, and hindered, looking into the field of potential, but just need to be free and delivered.

In this book, my goal is to provide some revelation and shed some light on the subject of deliverance. Many don't want to talk about it because there are people who make others feel shame for needing it. But trust me – at some point, all of us have needed or will need to be delivered from something. You chose the right book, and now you are on the path of mental, spiritual, and physical freedom. Let's jump right into it. Time is very valuable, so turn the page.

Chapter 1

✝

YOU GOT DOMINION

First of all, it is important for you to understand that it is the will of God for you to be delivered. We were not created to be dominated or controlled by anything. It is the idea of the Father that we in fact dominate everything.

Let's consider the word:

And God said, Let us make man in our image, after our likeness: and let them have dominion over the fish of the sea, and over the fowl of the air, and over the cattle, and over all the earth, and over every creeping thing that creepeth upon the earth. So God created man in his own image, in the image of God created he him; male and female created he them. And God blessed them, and God

said unto them, Be fruitful, and multiply, and replen-
ish the earth, and subdue it: and have dominion over the
fish of the sea, and over the fowl of the air, and over
every living thing that moveth upon the earth.
(Genesis 1:26-28)

The word He uses in verse 26 means **dominion**. The Hebrew word is **Re'dah**, which means *"having the power to rule and dominate"*. What I like about the text is that it specifies "over every living thing that moveth upon the earth". Guess what that means – the natural and the spiritual. That covers all the kingdoms that operate in the spirit and earth realms because everything is living.

So it only makes sense to give them (male and female) dominion over everything that's "living", even though at this time they didn't have to use or exercise their dominion over evil because the portal of evil was not open just yet. They were exposed to evil in chapter 3 after disobeying a direct command from God in chapter 2. Make no mistake: evil had already existed. God Himself created it! But just because he created it, it doesn't mean they had to be exposed to it.

Let's take a look:

I form the light, and create darkness: I make peace, and create evil: I the Lord do all these things. (Isaiah 45:7)

And the Lord God took the man, and put him into the garden of Eden to dress it and to keep it. And the Lord

God commanded the man, saying, Of every tree of the garden thou mayest freely eat: But of the tree of the knowledge of good and evil, thou shalt not eat of it: for in the day that thou eatest thereof thou shalt surely die. (Genesis 2:15-17)

And the serpent said unto the woman, Ye shall not surely die: For God doth know that in the day ye eat thereof, then your eyes shall be opened, and ye shall be as gods, knowing good and evil. And when the woman saw that the tree was good for food, and that it was pleasant to the eyes, and a tree to be desired to make one wise, she took of the fruit thereof, and did eat, and gave also unto her husband with her; and he did eat. And the eyes of them both were opened, and they knew that they were naked; and they sewed fig leaves together, and made themselves aprons. (Genesis 3:4-7)

Disobedience always gives the kingdom of darkness access to your life. Now, at this point, humanity has lost authority and dominion because of lack of obedience. Having dominion over the animal kingdom was the basic, practical application of dominion over something they could see, but when something they couldn't see showed up, they could summon the same power and authority for any given situation.

Satan couldn't approach them in the Spirit just yet because the gates of hell were not open just yet. Jesus talks about the gates of hell in the writings of Matthew:

And I say also unto thee, That thou art Peter, and upon this rock I will build my church; and the gates of hell shall not prevail against it. (Matthew 16:18)

Satan approached Eve in the body of a serpent. Why? He knew they had dominion over the animal kingdom, so if he could get them to disobey God within the scope of the familiar authority they had, this would break down the wall of all authority and dominion, and he could find a foothold and gain access to their lives. This was, in fact, the first recorded possession of a body of any kind when

Satan operated through a snake. God gave Adam and Eve a picture of what it was like to be possessedby a demon. He showed them Satan's limitation in that he could only possess animals and not humans,especially those who were full of God.

However, they missed the revelation. Perhaps their discernment was off.

Why do I say that? It's because they engaged in social intercoursewith a demon using the body of a snake and didn't even know it. This opened the door for man to be possessed when, at one time, it had been impossible.

How do we get dominion and authority back? They have to come through the last Adam, which is Jesus. Jesus' death, burial, and resurrection gave back our access to the power and authority we lost through the first Adam. Hallelujah! Glory to the Lamb of God!

Let's look into it:

And being found in fashion as a man, he humbled himself, and became obedient unto death, even the death of the cross. Wherefore God also hath highly exalted him, and given him a name which is above every name: That at the name of Jesus every knee should bow, of things in heaven, and things in earth, and things under the earth; And that every tongue should confess that Jesus Christ is Lord, to the glory of God the Father.
(Philippians 2:8-11)

So it's safe to say that both the living and the dead are under the authority of Jesus Christ!

Let's go deeper:

And what is the exceeding greatness of his power to us-ward who believe, according to the working of his mighty power, Which he wrought in Christ, when he raised him from the dead, and set him at his own right hand in the heavenly places, Far above all principality, and power, and might, and dominion, and every name that is named, not only in this world, but also in that which is to come... (Ephesians 1:19-21)

The word has made it clear that Jesus has power-er and authority over all principalities, powers, and dominions of this world and the world to come.

Who is gone into heaven, and is on the right hand of God; angels and authorities and powers being made subject unto him. (1 Peter 3:22)

You may be thinking, So, what does that have to do with me?

That has everything to do with you because that same power and authority have been transferred to you. That's why when you become a real follower of Christ, the devil doesn't like you and in some ways is afraid of you. The ones he's not afraid of are the ones who don't know what I'm teaching you in this book. The lack of knowledge has caused many to live a defeated live.

My people are destroyed for lack of knowledge: because thou hast rejected knowledge, I will also reject thee, that thou shalt be no priest to me... (Hosea 4:6)

However, I want you to declare the following as you read this book: "In the name of Jesus, I'm getting my life back!"

Now declare this: "I have power and authority in every area of my life in Jesus' name!"

Now that you have declared it, let me show you that what was in Jesus has been transferred to you so that it will cause somebody else's transformation to happen.

Behold, I give unto you power to tread on serpents and scorpions, and over all the power of the enemy: and nothing shall by any means hurt you. (Luke 10:19)

The word "power" in Greek is exousia, which means "the power of authority and/or a ruler of a government". It's as if Jesus were telling us, "I'm giving you power and authority to rule as a governor." What is a governor? It's someone who exercises authority over an area. So, what's our area or territory? The earth realm belongs to us to rule. Guess what— Jesus gives us the power and authority that we need to function like God intended in Genesis 1:26.

The heaven, even the heavens, are the Lord's: but the earth hath he given to the children of men.
(Psalm 115:16)

Some may be thinking, What about the spirit realm? Do we have some authority in the realm of the spirit? Yes, indeed! As a matter of fact, Jesus shows us how to operate in the Spirit, and what's done in the Spirit will have an earthly effect as well.

Let's take a look at a few verses in Matthew 16:

And I say also unto thee, That thou art Peter, and upon this rock I will build my church; and the gates of hell shall not prevail against it. And I will give unto thee the keys of the kingdom of heaven: and whatsoever thou shalt bind on earth shall be bound in heaven: and whatsoever thou shalt loose on earth shall be loosed in heaven.
(Matthew 16:18-19)

Jesus said you have keys to this realm! Anybody with keys to a place has some kind of authority. He said you can stop what you don't want and release what you do want. As believers, it's time to use what Jesus died for us to have. No more living a defeated life and just accepting the attacks from the enemy as normal experiences. No, bind him and loose in your life what you want. Come on, governor, you have the authority! Now, let's get free.

Rhema Notes

_____

_____

_____

_____

_____

_____

_____

_____

_____

_____

_____

_____

_____

_____

_____

_____

_____

_____

_____

RHEMA NOTES

Carlos Turner

Rhema Notes

_____

_____

_____

_____

_____

_____

_____

_____

_____

_____

_____

_____

_____

_____

_____

_____

_____

_____

_____

_____

_____

_____

_____

_____

_____

_____

_____

_____

_____

_____

RHEMA NOTES

_____
_____
_____
_____
_____
_____
_____
_____
_____
_____
_____
_____
_____
_____
_____
_____
_____
_____
_____
_____
_____
_____
_____
_____
_____
_____
_____
_____
_____

RHEMA NOTES

_____

_____

_____

_____

_____

_____

_____

_____

_____

_____

_____

_____

_____

_____

_____

_____

_____

_____

_____

_____

_____

_____

_____

_____

_____

_____

_____

_____

Chapter 2

✝

DELIVERANCE: "STRONGHOLDS"

"For the weapons of our warfare are not carnal, but mighty through God to the pulling down of strongholds..." (2 Corinthians 10:4)

The experience that is used to introduce us to divine freedom is called **deliverance** or being **delivered**. Just like I said in my introduction, everybody at some point has been delivered or needed deliverance. Either way, it's a blessing to be introduced to a freedom and be able to cut ourselves off from bondage and slavery.

If the Son therefore shall make you free, ye shall be free indeed. (John 8:36)

What gets me excited is knowing God's love is stronger than any stronghold that the enemy uses to try to hold me down. Amen!

It was in the late 80s. I was in my teens. My family and I attended a church called Promise Land COG-IC in Osceola, Arkansas. We would have great revivalists come through the city and be used mightily by the Lord. One time, while playing the drums during an altar call, I heard a loud scream. I was like, "It's all cool. She's just feeling the Spirit." All of a sudden, I saw the church mothers gathering around this woman, namely two powerful evangelist women, Eula Jackson and Ann Tunstall.

They began to say things like, "Loose your holt! Right now, loose your holt, Satan!"

The woman started hollering louder, rolling on the floor, and they continued to say, "Loose here! Now, come out!"

Yes, you guessed it: the woman was delivered from a demonic force!

I must be honest. At first, I didn't understand why they would use certain words to make certain things happen in the Spirit, but God later gave me wisdom about deliverance. What I learned was deliverance happens in stages. The Lord explained to me that when they would say, "Loose your holt!", they really meant "hold". This is the first thing you have to do in helping somebody get delivered. The stronghold has to be broken and destroyed before the demon can ever leave. A demon isn't going to leave if he still has a good grip on your soul.

What is the soul?

It's the will, mind, and emotions of a man. God shared with me that many try to call Him out without dealing with the stronghold, which in fact takes up more time because of a lack of spiritual knowledge.

I remember when I was a little boy, and I was bad and always getting a whooping for something. This one time, I had done something crazy, and my mama said, "Go get the belt, and hurry up!" First of all, I wasn't getting in any hurry to get a whooping. I was going to walk as slowly as possible going to get the belt. If I took too long, she would come in the room and get the belt, and I would hold the door for dear life. She would try to pull me off, but I would get a better grip, and before long, she'd get tired of dealing with me and let me go. I am telling you that story because that's how the devil operates. He gets a grip and establishes a stronghold, and eventually we get tired of dealing with him, so we leave him alone. But after reading this book, praise the Lord! Millions are about to get free in Jesus' name.

The question is: what is a stronghold? And what does the word have to say about it?

For the weapons of our warfare are not carnal, but mighty through God to the pulling down of strongholds... (2 Corinthians 10:4)

Paul said we have weapons of warfare that possess the power to pull down strongholds. Now, let me clear something up. If you are dealing with a stronghold, you are in a spiritual war. It's not going to be easy, but with God, all things are possible (Luke 1:37).

Let's take a look at the text because this is the first stage to getting delivered. Most are trying to call the demon out before dealing with the stronghold. This is a major mistake! The stronghold must be dealt with, and Paul was teaching the Corinthian church it must be pulled down.

The word "stronghold" comes from the Greek word *ochuroma*; one definition provided for this word is *"to brace and hold one down safely"*. Another definition is *"to rely upon"*. It's safe to say that a stronghold is something that braces one down by making them feel safe and able while relying on it.

That's something serious, would you not agree? The enemy is so crafty that he would make you feel safe while your life is in a mess. As long as you are relying on the stronghold, you will have no problems with the enemy. But the moment you decide that you are ready to be free, he'll do all he can to tighten up the grip.

Paul said they need to be pulled down. What does the phrase "pull down" mean? The phrase "pull down" comes from the Greek word *kathairesia*, which means *"to demolish"* or *"to destroy"*. So, strongholds not only need to be broken, but they also need to destroyed. It's not the will of the Father that we should stay in bondage of any kind! I praise God that He has made a way for me to escape.

There hath no temptation taken you but such as is common to man: but God is faithful, who will not suffer you to be tempted above that ye are able; but will with the temptation also make a way to escape, that ye may be able to bear it. (1 Corinthians 10:13)

Before you start calling demons out of people, make sure you deal with the stronghold first. If you know you have a stronghold, first you must confront it. Secondly, you must confess it. Thirdly, you conquer it! This is the hour of visitation. Chains are being broken now in Jesus' name!

Rhema Notes

_____

_____

_____

_____

_____

_____

_____

_____

_____

_____

_____

_____

_____

_____

_____

_____

Rhema Notes

_____

_____

_____

_____

_____

_____

_____

_____

_____

_____

_____

_____

_____

_____

_____

_____

_____

_____

_____

_____

_____

_____

_____

_____

_____

_____

_____

RHEMA NOTES

_____
_____
_____
_____
_____
_____
_____
_____
_____
_____
_____
_____
_____
_____
_____
_____
_____
_____
_____
_____
_____
_____
_____
_____
_____
_____
_____
_____

Carlos Turner

Rhema Notes

RHEMA NOTES

_____

_____

_____

_____

_____

_____

_____

_____

_____

_____

_____

_____

_____

_____

_____

_____

_____

_____

_____

_____

_____

_____

_____

_____

_____

_____

_____

RHEMA NOTES

Chapter 3

✝

DELIVERANCE: "YOU AIN'T GOTTA GO HOME, BUT YOU GOTTA LEAVE HERE!"

Behold, I give unto you power to tread on serpents and scorpions, and over all the power of the enemy: and nothing shall by any means hurt you. (Luke 10:19)

Now that we have some wisdom about the first stage of deliverance, let's deal with the second stage. One of the main reasons demons don't leave or move on is because of the Spirit of Fear. This spirit keeps us paralyzed and unable to flow in spiritual things. It keeps us safe. I tell people everywhere I go: you can't live a supernatural life trying to stay safe. When operating in the things of the Spirit, one must take both calculated and noncalculated risks. Fear has robbed us long enough.

Let's consider the word:

For God hath not given us the spirit of fear; but of power, and of love, and of a sound mind. (2 Timothy 1:7)

Fear fights three things that come from God:

1. POWER– The word "power" comes from the Greek word *dunamis,* which means *"an inherent ability to perform miracles".* Fear fights against our ability to operate in power. Why? Because it opens the door to disobedience, and somebody's miracle is in our obedience. Obedience itself produces power.

2. LOVE– The word "love" comes from the Greek word *agape,* which means *"an unconditional brotherly affection for another".* This is a major problem in the body of Christ. Fear has caused many to limit their love for each other. Why? Because we have a tendency to judge each other due to our previous experiences. So, when it's time to help, give, uplift, or minister to others, fear reminds us of our last bad experience, and we miss an opportunity to be used by God. The highest representation of God is love.

3. MIND– The word "mind" comes from the Greek word *sophronismos,* which means *"to have one's senses in check"* or *"to have self-control".* Your senses are the control center for the Spirit of Fear. If we are going to do great things for God, we must walk by faith and not by our senses. God has given us a "sound" mind, which means having discipline over one's senses. Glory to God!

So, as we can see, we have everything we need to overcome every strategy of the enemy. That's good news! Paul reminds us to put on the whole armor of God. Why? So we stand against the trickery of the devil.

Let's take a look at Ephesians chapter 6:

Put on the whole armour of God, that ye may be able to stand against the wiles of the devil. For we wrestle not against flesh and blood, but against principalities, against powers, against the rulers of the darkness of this world, against spiritual wickedness in high places. Wherefore take unto you the whole armour of God, that ye may be able to withstand in the evil day, and having done all, to stand. Stand therefore, having your loins girt about with truth, and having on the breastplate of righteousness; And your feet shod with the preparation of the gospel of peace; Above all, taking the shield of faith, wherewith ye shall be able to quench all the fiery darts of the wicked. And take the helmet of salvation, and the sword of the Spirit, which is the word of God...
(Ephesians 6:11-17)

Let's look at the phrase "wiles of the devil". In the Greek, the word "wiles" is ***methodeia***, which is where we get our English word "method".

The word *methodeia* means *"deceit or trickery"*. The enemy will try anything and everything to throw you off and keep your mind off of him. When holiness is our focus, we have an assignment to shine a light in every dark place in our lives. Amen!

It is not God's will for us to be overtaken by a demon or evil spirit of any kind. We have the power to cast them out. If you have a demon, you need to get connected with somebody who operates in apostolic power, and you can be free in Jesus' name.

Jesus didn't play with the kingdom of darkness. He cast out devils, period! Jesus is our example.

If Jesus did it, and if he is our example, we are supposed to do it. As a matter of fact, he told us to do it so the kingdom of Heaven can be demonstrated.

And as ye go, preach, saying, The kingdom of heaven is at hand. Heal the sick, cleanse the lepers, raise the dead, cast out devils: freely ye have received, freely give.
(Matthew 10:7-8)

He instructed them to cast out devils. In other words, he instructed them to make deliverance available to the people so they could be free. When Jesus called on his twelve disciples, he told them to preach, heal, and cast out devils. He ordained them to operate in a healing and deliverance ministry.

Let's take a look:

And he goeth up into a mountain, and calleth unto him whom he would: and they came unto him. And he ordained twelve, that they should be with him, and that he might send them forth to preach, And to have power to heal sicknesses, and to cast out devils: And Simon he surnamed Peter; And James the son of Zebedee, and John the brother of James; and he surnamed them Boanerges, which is, The sons of thunder: And Andrew, and Philip, and Bartholomew, and Matthew, and Thomas, and James the son of Alphaeus, and Thaddaeus, and Simon the Canaanite, and Judas Iscariot, which also betrayed him: and they went into an house. (Mark 3:13-19)

We don't see this as often now. This is a much needed ministry in the body of Christ. Most focus on the preaching. Let me be clear: we have the best preachers and orators, but they have put the deliverance element on the backburner. I believe God is raising up a body of people who will pay the price and make sacrifices in order to see the people of God healed, delivered, and set free.

RHEMA NOTES

_____
_____
_____
_____
_____

Carlos Turner

RHEMA NOTES

RHEMA NOTES

_____
_____
_____
_____
_____
_____
_____
_____
_____
_____
_____
_____
_____
_____
_____
_____
_____
_____
_____
_____
_____
_____
_____
_____
_____
_____

Rhema Notes

_____

_____

_____

_____

_____

_____

_____

_____

_____

_____

_____

_____

_____

_____

_____

_____

_____

_____

_____

_____

_____

_____

_____

_____

_____

_____

_____

_____

RHEMA NOTES

_____

_____

_____

_____

_____

_____

_____

_____

_____

_____

_____

_____

_____

_____

_____

_____

_____

_____

_____

_____

_____

_____

_____

_____

_____

_____

_____

_____

_____

Rhema Notes

_____

_____

_____

_____

_____

_____

_____

_____

_____

_____

_____

_____

_____

_____

_____

_____

_____

_____

_____

_____

_____

_____

_____

_____

_____

_____

_____

_____

_____

_____

Chapter 4

†

DELIVERANCE:
GET THIS RESIDUE OFF OF ME

Lest Satan should get an advantage of us: for we are not ignorant of his devices. (2 Corinthians 2:11)

I'm not much of a fisherman, but one spring weekend, I decided to go out with a few fellows to fish. I really thought I was doing something. I had my license, my rod, and my bait. I was out there for hours and didn't catch a thing. The brothers were catching everything, but not this preacher! Of course, I was the joke of the day, but I told them, "I am a fisher of men. I can go and buy fish!" They were so tickled, but I was so serious. We were loading up and heading home. Mind you, I didn't catch anything, but I was around those who had caught everything. I got back to my car, and I drove off. I got a call from my son, asking me to pick him up from the gym.

When I arrived and he got in the car, he asked, "Dad, what's that smell?"

"Nothing!" I said. I always kept a clean car.

"It smells like fish in your car!"

"That's not possible," I said. I didn't catch anything or touch anything.

"Dad, I'm serious," he said. "It smells like fish in here."

And then it hit me: even though I didn't catch the fish or touch the fish, I still smelled like fish because the environment I was in left a fishy residual smell on me.

That's how it is after the first two stages of deliverance; although you don't do what you used to do, the residue of what you used to do is still on you. So, this leads up to stage 3. The third stage is to ask God to remove the residue of what you were before! I want this to be clear that just because you have been renewed and transformed in the Spirit, it doesn't mean your flesh got saved. Your flesh will never get saved!

Let's take a look at the scripture:

For whosoever shall call upon the name of the Lord shall be saved. (Romans 10:13)

Therefore if any man be in Christ, he is a new creature: old things are passed away; behold, all things are become new.
(2 Corinthians 5:17)

Let's look at the word "creature". It comes from the Greek word ***ktisis***, which means *"an institution"*. When you are converted, you are immediately in covenant with God, which makes it an institution. So, it's safe to say that to become a new creature is to be involved in a better covenant that has better promises. Glory to God!

But now hath he obtained a more excellent ministry, by how much also he is the mediator of a better covenant, which was established upon better promises.
(Hebrews 8:6)

So, as we can see, God deals with our inner man, and that's what we need to work on daily as well.

That he would grant you, according to the riches of his glory, to be strengthened with might by his Spirit in the inner man... (Ephesians 3:16)

As the Father continues to strengthen our spirits, we must consider we still have flesh to deal with. This is the area where the residue remains.

For I know that in me (that is, in my flesh,) dwelleth no good thing: for to will is present with me; but how to perform that which is good I find not. (Romans 7:18)

This is why it is so important to have a prayer life! Those who don't have a prayer life, especially in this last hour, are not going to make it.

Prayer is the key to making it in this last hour.

Pray without ceasing. (1 Thessalonians 5:17)

The enemy will do whatever he has to do to keep tabs on you and your destiny. Jesus lays out Satan's plans in the book of John.

The thief cometh not, but for to steal, and to kill, and to destroy: I am come that they might have life, and that they might have it more abundantly. (John 10:10)

So, as we can see, we have to fight for our lives every day. We are in a war, and the devil doesn't want us to win. When an evil spirit is cast out of a physical body, if that person is not filled with the Holy Spirit and the word, that spirit will come back because the residue of him being there is still on that individual. This happens because what had been there has not been replaced with what should be there. Demons can't legally stay on the earth unless they find a physical body to dwell in. So, even if deliverance did take place, if there's still residue and there's no word to fight off the enemy, that demon will return with more demons worse than himself.

Let's look into it:

When the unclean spirit is gone out of a man, he walketh through dry places, seeking rest, and findeth none. Then he saith, I will return into my house from whence I came out; and when he is come, he findeth it empty, swept, and garnished. Then goeth he, and taketh with himself seven other spirits more wicked than himself, and they enter in and dwell there: and the last state of that man is worse than the first. Even so shall it be also unto this wicked generation. (Matthew 12:43-45)

The third stage of deliverance is just as important as the first. Familiar spirits create an atmosphere that makes you feel comfortable with your residue, not knowing you are a spiritual red flag that still needs some deliverance. It's also worth noting concerning the text that the goal of the enemy is to open a door for a team of demons to live in you. That's right – an organized team! His agenda is to get a demonic organization established within you so that the team of demons can run you like a business.

Listen, beloved. This is no game. This is serious business! That's why we must be about God's business.

Now, when residue stays on you for too long, what happens, for believers especially, is that we become lukewarm. We start to lose our desire for the things of God and compromise just to feel a part of something. As a lukewarm person, you are neither hot nor cold, so the standard of living is lowered, which then makes you feel comfortable in the state you are in.

John addresses this very thing in his appeal to the Laodicean church:

He that hath an ear, let him hear what the Spirit saith unto the churches. And unto the angel of the church of the Laodiceans write; These things saith the Amen, the faithful and true witness, the beginning of the creation of God; I know thy works, that thou art neither cold nor hot: I would thou wert cold or hot. So then because thou art lukewarm, and neither cold nor hot, I will spue thee out of my mouth. (Revelation 3:13-16)

I was once told to never start something that I couldn't finish. This is a truth that relates to deliverance. You have to finish the process and get all of it out and off. We can't afford to be full of the devil but still attempting to speak for God.

Declare this with me: "God, get it all out and get it all off!" In Jesus' name. Amen!

Rhema Notes

_____

_____

_____

_____

_____

_____

_____

_____

_____

_____

_____

_____

Rhema Notes

_____

_____

_____

_____

_____

_____

_____

_____

_____

_____

_____

_____

_____

_____

_____

_____

_____

_____

_____

_____

_____

_____

_____

_____

_____

_____

_____

_____

_____

_____

_____

_____

_____

RHEMA NOTES

_____

_____

_____

_____

_____

_____

_____

_____

_____

_____

_____

_____

_____

_____

_____

_____

_____

_____

_____

_____

_____

_____

_____

_____

_____

_____

_____

RHEMA NOTES

_____

_____

_____

_____

_____

_____

_____

_____

_____

_____

_____

_____

_____

_____

_____

_____

_____

_____

_____

_____

_____

_____

_____

_____

_____

_____

_____

_____

_____

_____

_____

_____

_____

_____

Carlos Turner

Rhema Notes

_____
_____
_____
_____
_____
_____
_____
_____
_____
_____
_____
_____
_____
_____
_____
_____
_____
_____
_____
_____
_____
_____
_____
_____
_____
_____
_____
_____

RHEMA NOTES

_____

_____

_____

_____

_____

_____

_____

_____

_____

_____

_____

_____

_____

_____

_____

_____

_____

_____

_____

_____

_____

_____

_____

_____

_____

_____

_____

_____

_____

_____

_____

_____

RHEMA NOTES

Chapter 5

✝

LIVING FREE

Stand fast therefore in the liberty wherewith Christ hath made us free, and be not entangled again with the yoke of bondage. (Galatians 5:1)

I am reminded of a story about a dog chained to a tree in a neighborhood. Every day, adults and kids alike bothered the dog. They got really close, hit him on the head with a stick, and backed up just enough so he couldn't harm them. This went on for years. It went on for so long that the kids drew a line in the ground to show how far the dog could go. One day, the owner looked out from his front room window and decided to play ball with his dog. He unhooked him from the tree and took the chain off his neck. The owner of the dog took a tennis ball and threw it to the other side of the yard. The dog got excited, barked, ran, and then stopped. The owner went and got the ball, came back, and threw the ball. The dog got excited, ran from the tree again, but stopped again. The owner went over to where his dog was and realized the dog had stopped at the very place the kids drew a line in the dirt. He quickly realized that his dog had been chained for so long that he didn't know he was free. The dog's mind had been conditioned to only go so far because of the bondage he was once in.

This is a great example of how many operate and function today. God has released us from chains and bondage, but we are still living like people in slavery. So, just like the owner of the dog learned that he had to retrain the mind of his dog, we too have to retrain our minds so we can start living in freedom.

Let's deal with the mind because the mind is the starting place to your freedom. The Bible says that, without your mind, you couldn't do anything.

But without thy mind would I do nothing; that thy benefit should not be as it were of necessity, but willingly. (Philemon 1:14)

We need our minds to shift in and out of experiences in life. The mind is a powerful gift from God. He ends seasons in our lives and introduces new seasons in our lives. This is the main reason why the enemy fights constantly against our minds. The enemy knows once you get your mind right, things will start to fall into place. Many thank God for material things, but we need to thank God for our minds. If you are in bondage, your thinking is off, which causes you to make decisions that are not healthy for your destiny.

Jesus cast out a demon in a man, and after the deliverance, the Bible shares with us that he was not only delivered, but he had his mind back.

And they came over unto the other side of the sea, into the country of the Gadarenes. And when he was come out of the ship, immediately there met him out of the tombs a man with an unclean spirit, Who had his dwelling among the tombs; and no man could bind him, no, not with chains: Because that he had been often bound with fetters and chains, and the chains had been plucked asunder by him, and the fetters broken in pieces: neither could any man tame him. And always, night and day, he was in the mountains, and in the tombs, crying, and cutting himself with stones. But when he saw Jesus afar off, he ran and worshipped him, And cried with a loud voice, and said, What have I to do with thee, Jesus, thou Son of the most high God? I adjure thee by God, that thou torment me not. For he said unto him, Come out of the man, thou unclean spirit. And he asked him, What is thy name? And he answered, saying, My name is Legion: for we are many. And he besought him much that he would not send them away out of the country. Now there was there nigh unto the mountains a great herd of swine feeding. And all the devils besought him, saying, Send us into the swine, that we may enter into them.

And forthwith Jesus gave them leave. And the unclean spirits went out, and entered into the swine: and the herd ran violently down a steep place into the sea, (they were about two thousand;) and were choked in the sea. And they that fed the swine fled, and told it in the city, and in the country. And they went out to see what it was that was done. And they come to Jesus, and see him that was possessed with the devil, and had the legion, sitting, and clothed, and in his right mind: and they were afraid.
(Mark 5:1-15)

Take a moment right where you are and say, "Lord, I thank you for my mind." Amen!

Let's go deeper:

For as he thinketh in his heart, so is he: Eat and drink, saith he to thee; but his heart is not with thee.
(Proverbs 23:7)

The word "heart" comes from the Hebrew word **nephesh,** and one definition for that word is *"mind"*. As a man thinks in his mind, so is he! So, it's safe to say we are what we think about all the time. That's why it's important to be around those who make deposits in your life instead of withdrawals from your life all the time. Also, if you are around negative people, it's going to affect you negatively, and it works the same way as it relates to positive people. The mind is a powerful gift.

Paul was teaching the Philippian church, sharing

with them what kind of mind to have.

Let's take a look:

If there be therefore any consolation in Christ, if any comfort of love, if any fellowship of the Spirit, if any bowels and mercies, Fulfil ye my joy, that ye be like-minded, having the same love, being of one accord, of one mind. Let nothing be done through strife or vainglory; but in lowliness of mind let each esteem other better than themselves. Look not every man on his own things, but every man also on the things of others. Let this mind be in you, which was also in Christ Jesus: Who, being in the form of God, thought it not robbery to be equal with God... (Philippians 2:1-6)

Paul gives us a list of things to create a foundation for how our minds should be. I love verse 5 because he shares that Jesus had the same mind that he was teaching them about. Likewise, we should, too. The mind of Christ doesn't come automatically. It comes through a process that involves hard work.

Let's look in the word:

I beseech you therefore, brethren, by the mercies of God, that ye present your bodies a living sacrifice, holy, acceptable unto God, which is your reasonable service. And be not conformed to this world: but be ye transformed by the renewing of your mind, that ye may prove what is

that good, and acceptable, and perfect, will of God.
(Romans 12:1-2)

He teaches in verse 2 not to be conformed to this world. The word "conformed" comes from the Greek word **suschematizo**, which means *"to fashion oneself according to and/or operate within the same patterns"*. Paul is saying not to walk in the patterns presented to you from the world. We are in the world, but we are not of the world. We live and operate within the Kingdom of God. We cannot afford to adapt to the world's ways in order to be accepted by our peers. We must stand firm, trust God, and stay in alignment with those things that represent the Kingdom. Amen!

In the next passage, Paul shares with us how to not conform. He says, "Be ye transformed by the renewing of your mind", so it's safe to say that transformation is a process. It takes daily renewing of the mind.

The word "renewing" comes from the Greek word **anakainosis**, which means *"a complete renovation"*. What's interesting about the word "renewing" is that it suggests continuation. There must be a continual renewal of the mind when seasons change for you. You can't function in a "last season" mindset while trying to do new things. If you stay in a certain season too long without renewing your mind, conforming to this world is most likely going to happen.

You have to shift if you are going to live free.

As we can see, it's so important to have our minds right if we are going to walk in a freedom anointing.

No chains, no handcuffs, no shackles, no straitjacket –just peace because freedom is the mother of peace.

Now the question is: how do I renew my mind? Is it in the Bible? Yes, it is!

Let's take a look:

And the peace of God, which passeth all understanding, shall keep your hearts and minds through Christ Jesus. Finally, brethren, whatsoever things are true, whatsoever things are honest, whatsoever things are just, whatsoever things are pure, whatsoever things are lovely, whatsoever things are of good report; if there be any virtue, and if there be any praise, think on these things. (Phillippians 4:7-8)

This is how we keep our minds right and our hearts pure. He tells us to think on these things. The word "think" comes from the Greek word *logizomai*, which actually means *"to calculate and to compute inwardly"*. If we would spend time thinking or computing in our minds about honesty, justice, purity, love, good news (instead of bad news), excellence, and honor, this world would be a much better place. This should be our daily mental appetite in order to stay free and walk in divine peace.

Carlos Turner

Rhema Notes

RHEMA NOTES

_____

_____

_____

_____

_____

_____

_____

_____

_____

_____

_____

_____

_____

_____

_____

_____

_____

_____

_____

_____

_____

_____

_____

_____

_____

_____

_____

_____

_____

_____

_____

Rhema Notes

RHEMA NOTES

_____
_____
_____
_____
_____
_____
_____
_____
_____
_____
_____
_____
_____
_____
_____
_____
_____
_____
_____
_____
_____
_____
_____
_____
_____
_____
_____
_____
_____
_____
_____
_____

Rhema Notes

RHEMA NOTES

_____

_____

_____

_____

_____

_____

_____

_____

_____

_____

_____

_____

_____

_____

_____

_____

_____

_____

_____

_____

_____

_____

_____

_____

_____

_____

_____

_____

_____

Rhema Notes

_____

_____

_____

_____

_____

_____

_____

_____

_____

_____

_____

_____

_____

_____

_____

_____

_____

_____

_____

_____

_____

_____

_____

_____

_____

_____

_____

_____

_____

_____

_____

_____

CONCLUSION

One of my desires for the body of Christ is to see churches across the globe operating in a deliverance ministry. No matter the church name or affiliation, people around the world are in dire need of help and deliverance.

Obadiah 1:17 says, "But upon mount Zion shall be deliverance, and there shall be holiness; and the house of Jacob shall possess their possessions." We can see there's a clear connection between holiness, deliverance, and possession. As we all know, holiness is not preached today like it was when I came up, but God is still calling for the body of Christ to be and to live holy. In Leviticus 11:45, He says, "For I am the Lord that bringeth you up out of the land of Egypt, to be your God: ye shall therefore be holy, for I am holy."

Why holiness, you may ask? He says in His word that He brought them out of Egypt, which represents bondage, to be their God and for them to be holy. Why? Because He is holy! Holiness is the master key to staying delivered. When holiness is the focus, deliverance is not required. Now, after the children of Israel experienced deliverance, they had full ownership of their possessions. Alleluia!

I wrote this book in obedience to the Father to tell you personally that it's time for you to take ownership of your possessions. See Exodus chapter 12. God loves us, and He wants all of us to be free. There's nothing wrong with needing deliverance, but there is something wrong when you are too blind to admit it.

As we continue to seek the will of the Father, may His hands be upon you and may He guide you into all truth. I bless you, my brothers and sisters! May the Lord bless thee, may the Lord keep thee, may the Lord make His face shine upon thee and be gracious to thee, may the Lord lift up His countenance upon thee and give thee peace. Shalom and amen!

Rhema Notes

_____
_____
_____
_____
_____
_____
_____
_____
_____
_____
_____
_____
_____
_____
_____
_____

RHEMA NOTES

_____
_____
_____
_____
_____
_____
_____
_____
_____
_____
_____
_____
_____
_____
_____
_____
_____
_____
_____
_____
_____
_____
_____
_____
_____
_____
_____
_____
_____

Carlos Turner

RHEMA NOTES

_____
_____
_____
_____
_____
_____
_____
_____
_____
_____
_____
_____
_____
_____
_____
_____
_____
_____
_____
_____
_____
_____
_____
_____
_____
_____
_____
_____

Rhema Notes

_____

_____

_____

_____

_____

_____

_____

_____

_____

_____

_____

_____

_____

_____

_____

_____

_____

_____

_____

_____

_____

_____

_____

_____

_____

_____

_____

_____

_____

_____

Rhema Notes

_____

_____

_____

_____

_____

_____

_____

_____

_____

_____

_____

_____

_____

_____

_____

_____

_____

_____

_____

_____

_____

_____

_____

_____

_____

_____

_____

_____

_____

RHEMA NOTES

_____

_____

_____

_____

_____

_____

_____

_____

_____

_____

_____

_____

_____

_____

_____

_____

_____

_____

_____

_____

_____

_____

_____

_____

_____

_____

_____

_____

_____

_____

_____

_____

_____

Rhema Notes

ABOUT THE AUTHOR

APOSTLE **C. A. TURNER** is the prophetic voice for this last hour. He is the Senior Pastor and Founder of Kingdom Nation Ministries and About God's Business World Outreach ministries in Jonesboro, AR and Memphis, TN. He has been preaching and teaching for over 25 years, reaching the lost at all cost and impacting the earth with the things concerning the kingdom of God with miracles, signs, and wonders operating within his ministry. He attended Grambling State University with a focus in Business Administration. He also Attended the School of Exodus studying Theology and Biblical Studies. He is the founder of Y.E.S.S. Young Entrepreneur Success School for the urban youth with a focus in financial Literacy. Carlos Turner is the owner and CEO of several successful businesses, Kingdom Clean Detailing, Tojoe's Wings and Waffles, Turner and Thomas Real Estate, Carlo Avery Fashions, and Olive Tree Finance and Investment Firm. In his spare time, he loves reading, studying, and researching the things of the spirit to stay sharp and alert for the things to come! His favorite verse is found in the book of Luke 1:37 that says, "For with God nothing shall be impossible!" His assignment is to shake and reawaken the body of Christ in the area of the supernatural. He understands that this will be a life journey, so he is totally committed to the things of God and strictly being about God's Business.

Also Available from this Author

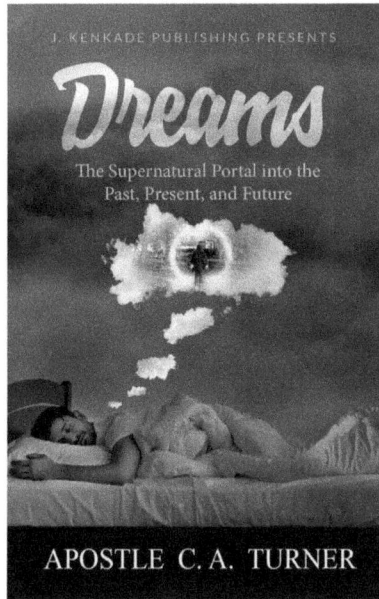

J. KENKADE PUBLISHING PRESENTS

Dreams

The Supernatural Portal into the
Past, Present, and Future

APOSTLE C. A. TURNER

ISBN: 978-1-944486-78-5
Visit www.amazon.com
Author: Apostle C. A. Turner

A study on the supernatural realm of Dreams, how God speaks to us
in our sleep, and what scripture has to say on this matter.

Also Available from this Author

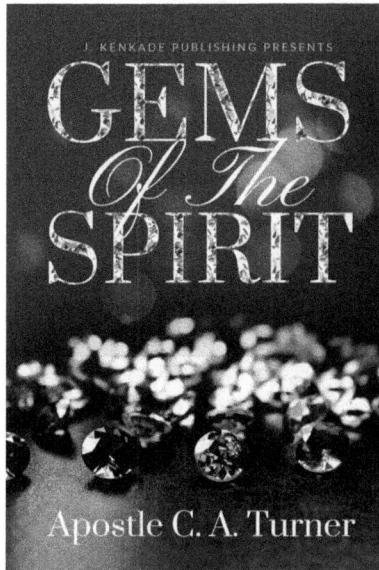

ISBN: 978-1-944486-83-9
Visit www.amazon.com
Author: Apostle C. A. Turner

There's such a hunger for the things of the spirit and the supernatural. Many have decided to tap into the dark side in order to understand more about the Supernatural and the things of the spirit. One of the reasons for this I believe, is because the church as a whole has lost the desire to see a move of God validated by his power with miracles, signs, and wonders. It's my desire and prayer that this information will activate you in ways you never dreamed as you apply it to your spiritual life.

Also Available from
J. Kenkade Publishing

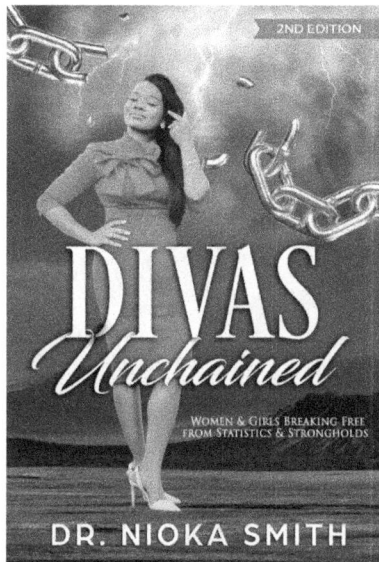

ISBN: 978-1-944486-25-9
Visit www.drniokasmith.com
Author: Dr. Nioka Smith

Sexually abused by her father at the age of 14, pregnant at the age of 17, and a nervous breakdown at the age of 28, Dr. Nioka Smith's painful past almost killed her, until the voice of the Lord guided her into destroying strongholds and reversing Satan's plan for her life. DIVAS Unchained is the powerful chain-breaking reality of the many unfortunate strongholds our women and girls face. Dr. Nioka uses her divine gift to help women and girls break free from destructive life cycles and prosper in all areas of life. Satan has lied to you. It's time to expose his lies. It's time to break free!

Also Available from
J. Kenkade Publishing

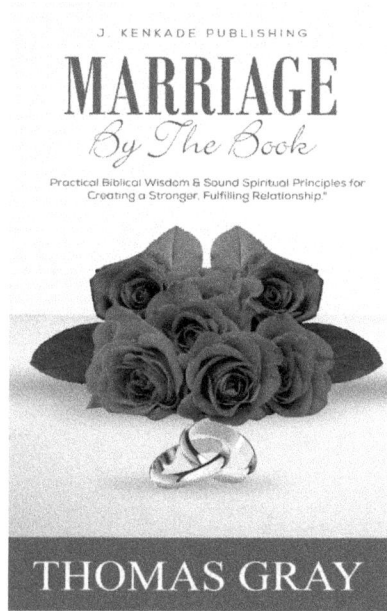

J. KENKADE PUBLISHING

MARRIAGE
By The Book

Practical Biblical Wisdom & Sound Spiritual Principles for
Creating a Stronger, Fulfilling Relationship."

THOMAS GRAY

ISBN: 978-1-944486-90-7
Visit www.amazon.com
Author: Pastor Thomas Gray

Marriage by the Book is a profound and practical guidebook de-
signed to help you cultivate a deeper relationship based on sound
Biblical wisdom. Written by Pastor Thomas Gray, this book com-
bines proven step-by-step strategies of practical relationships with
spiritual lessons and Bible-based principles to help you overcome
conflicts, improve your communication, handle difficult discus-
sions, and celebrate the unique union and covenant which unites
you together with God. Marriage by the Book is ideal for both
new and seasoned couples who are searching for better ways to
strengthen their relationship and fulfill their promises to God.
Pastor Thomas Gray: P.O. Box 360041/Dallas, TX 75336
www.twdcdaltx.org (972) 926-3762

Also Available from
J. Kenkade Publishing

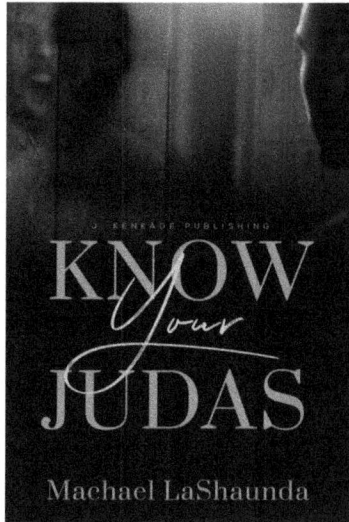

ISBN: 978-1-944486-26-6
Visit www.amazon.com
Author: Machael LaShaunda

Throughout life, we're always confronted with difficulty, but the deftness is learning how to name it, include it, and elevate from it. Studying the story of Judas, I realized it was at the proper time when Jesus rushed Judas away, the betrayal. Though He had the inside scoop on Judas, He didn't dismiss him to be rude, exclude him from the twelve, was frustrated, angry, or done with him. Jesus gave Judas the same anointing to heal the sick and to go out and teach. Judas watched Jesus preach, teach, and perform first-hand miracles even though Jesus knew the outcome of their relationship. No one is exempt from what in this book I will name as a Judas. Jesus wasn't the only One with a Judas. Moses had Pharaoh, David had Saul, Samson had Delilah, Naomi had grief and famine, Esther had Hamon, and the Woman with the issue of blood were all Judases. Know your Judas, an inspirational testament of the author is birthed from life encounters and learning how to overcome them. In this book, while reading the pages, it is important to be able to decipher your Judas, so your God given destiny is fulfilled and your purpose is no longer prolonged.

www.ingramcontent.com/pod-product-compliance
Lightning Source LLC
Chambersburg PA
CBHW060426090426
42734CB00011B/2461